21st Century Protests

A Handbook for Black America

Brooks B. Robinson

21st Century Protests: A Handbook for Black America

Printed in the United States of America

ISBN-13: 978-1535161350
ISBN-10: 1535161353

Dedication

To Walter, Xander, and Zora Bell, who we **hope** will never have to operationalize 21st century protests. However, if they do, then we **hope** that they will operationalize them with proficiency and vigor.

"**Hope**" is not a strategy. *21 Century **Protests*** can be an effective and successful strategy.

Preface

In order to motivate a divergence in historical cycles, it is often necessary to inject extraordinary events. Black Americans can see this when we recount our history in the Americas. We were able to help spur movement from slavery to "freedom" by engaging in passive protests—the Abolitionist Movement. While there was temporary progress during Reconstruction, there was a return to the near status quo with "Jim Crow" segregation in less than two decades. We were able to spur movement from "Jim Crow" segregation to the Civil Rights era through peaceful protests—the Civil Rights Movement. However, before two decades elapsed, efforts were already well underway to return to a near status quo and to thwart our progress with attacks on Affirmative Action, drug (crack cocaine) and viral (HIV) epidemics, and a surge in incarceration rates. Therefore, we stand nearly 60 years later in a position that is near to where we started. The most recent National Urban League report on our status (The *State of Black America*, 2016) indicates that we have made little progress with respect to our White counterparts over the past 40 years.[1] Yet we continue to operationalize another movement— Black Lives Matter—to stimulate a new round of "progress." However, history should tell us that no matter which gains are extracted from the system through peaceful agitation during the second decade of the 21st century, gains will only be permitted after plans have been devised to roll back the clock and make the gains of little-to-no effect in the long run.

When Black Americans "talk" about progress, we normally mean more income and wealth. At a minimum, we intend income, if not, wealth equality. At bottom, we comprehend

---

[1] The executive summary of the National Urban League's 2016 *State of Black America* puts forth this claim; http://soba.iamempowered.com/ (Retrieved May 23, 2016).

that green is the color that really matters in America. With green, you can obtain much of what you desire. Without green, "get back when you are Black." If we acknowledge that economic might makes right, then why do we continue to concentrate on peaceful and political means in our efforts to generate progressive change? If a house is made of sand, you can wash it away with water. However, if the house is made of stone, water will be of no effect in dislodging that house; you need a jack hammer, a wrecking ball, or dynamite.

Therefore, in an effort to open up the discussion about how to dislodge the American house of green and create real and lasting change for Black Americans, we provide this little book, *21st Century Protests: A Handbook for Black America*. It suggests several mainly economic paths (direct and indirect) for conducting protests that can be designed to help us get what we really want. It is somewhat out of context because, admittedly, we should settle on what we really want from America before we move forward with demands. Given that, as some say, there are really four Black Americas, it may be problematic to decide on a concise list of demands. Nevertheless, as we decide on a list of demands and move forward with our protests, we invite those organizing protests to consider what we believe are effective tools for helping force the larger nation to acquiesce and permit the smaller nation to take what we so richly deserve.

If we adopt methods from *21st Century Protests*, then we will be using appropriate methods for breaking the historical cycle and attacking an economic system that is, in its current form, designed to keep us at the bottom of the economic, social, and political ladder. If we do not adopt these methods, then we will not break the historical cycle and we are likely to see temporary gains that will be diffused later by actions that are designed to return us to a near status quo where Black Americans are, again, at the bottom.

Prologue

Protests are an important component of the US historical political landscape. You can peruse history books and see photographs of protest scenes throughout. Among those photographs, especially of well-written history books, will be photographs of Black Americans protesting to obtain freedom, civil rights, voting rights, and human rights. Even in 2016, one can imagine what future history books will portray assuming that they use photographs from today's newspapers of Black Lives Matter protests.

The problem with Black American protests, as we have written in response to a 2015 movie about one of the iconic protests, "Selma," our protests have too often been designed on the spur of the moment—making it up as we go along. Such absence of planning strategically means that we do not think long-term enough in order to make the best strategic decisions today.[2]

Hence, this book is designed to help us think about the type of real impact, economic protests that can be of long-lasting value to the canon of Black American protest types for the future. Let us seriously consider executing the types of economic protests outlined in this volume, which can help produce the types of outcomes that we desire. But before we undertake these protests, let us be certain that we know where we want to go into the future, one-hundred, two-hundred, and three-hundred years from now. Let us imagine what can be achieved if we make the correct strategic decisions and produce the outcomes that we desire. Let us discern what our posterity will say. Most importantly, let us act accordingly.

---

[2] See "'Selma': Lost Time. Lost Opportunity"; http://www.blackeconomics.org/BEMedia/Selma.pdf (Retrieved May 23, 2016).

Once we know where we want to go, these suggested economic protests and others that can be devised, can, without doubt, help us arrive at our desired destination.

Table of Contents

Introduction

There is something to be said for peaceful protests. When you are outnumbered six- or seven-to-one, then you may be well advised to attempt to negotiate peacefully to achieve your goals. (Notwithstanding those whose faith says that "He will support you with angels sufficient to ensure victory in battle.") However, when you are up against an obstinate opposition which has violence as its historical modus operandi, then you are very wise to seek to wrest political, social, and economic gains from the system using nonviolent physical approaches. That is not to say that you must avoid economic actions that can have significant and meaningful physical (monetary and fiscal) impacts.

Actually, Black Americans have been quite wise since the 1950s in this regard. Although we had the North Koreans, the North Vietnamese, and the Mau Mau among others, who proved that those in t-shirts, dungarees, and tennis shoes could fight strategically against those with big leather boots (the classic rice eaters versus beef eaters conflict), we decided to milk the system slowly with "peaceful protests."

Interestingly, we are engaged in one of the biggest con games in world history as we seek to convince White Americans that they have a duty to make us "equal." They used their brains, sweat, and brawn to steal North American lands; steal us from Africa; train us to be their good slaves; and they have used this physical and human capital to conquer the Earth world including the ocean depths, and much of our solar system. All along, it was quite clear that they intended to follow a key law: "self-preservation." Yet we refuse to see and hear that reality and are begging profusely to be given some of their returns. Yes, we helped generate those returns, but we seem oblivious to the fact that

1

we are only capitalist slave implements in the process. White Americans prove over and over again that they will only relent so much and only for so long before they impose their heavy-handed rule against problem makers. Economic and wealth equality, the only equality that really matters, is not a real option for Black Americans.

It is a con game because some of us think that we are slick enough to play on the conscious of White America to accept us as their sons and daughters. The reality is that the European is the inventor of the big con and cannot be conned. We must realize that we will forever be slaves in this system unless and until we decide to discontinue the con game, begin a nation building game, and develop our own system of life living.

Too much time, energy, and computer bytes have been, and are being, expended discussing the race issue. In the final analysis, most of what you have heard, seen, or read calls for peaceful protests that have little impact on the system. That is why there has been such limited progress since the Civil Rights Movement of the 1960s.[3] To a person, those who are leading the dialogue offer little-to-nothing of real substance that will actually change the way the world works because their strategy is not designed to attack the economic infrastructure. It is only by attacking the economic infrastructure that we can actually have a chance to create real change in our lives and for the lives of our posterity.

This book brings new strategies that Black Americans can use to create real change. This is not Obama change, and it

---

[3] Consider that a partial, yet significant, reason for the success of the Civil Rights Movement of the 1960s is the fact that it was buttressed by riots and organizations like Deacons for Defense and Justice and the Black Panther Party. In other words, peaceful demonstrations were coupled with the threat of, and actual, violence.

is not creating change the John Lewis way. The so-called American forefathers would be proud of this type of change; it is Boston Tea Party-type change. We are talking about creating change that can lead to Black Americans imposing our economic will on America, which will capture the attention of the capitalist plutocrats and oligarchs, who may be brought to a negotiating table that can produce Black American land as part of the just dessert.

The new protest strategies that we highlight have an economic focus. We not only present the strategies, but we also discuss the likely outcomes of implementing them. These are active strategies that embody certain pain for us, but greater pain for them. Unfortunately, Black Americans' situation is not dire enough at this time to motivate adoption of these strategies. However, the time will come when Black Americans will run to this little book seeking means to attack a system that egregiously and maliciously smashes those who oppose the status quo and who seek real freedom—"to do what we want the way we want."

This book analyzes the following 12 strategies that are designed to strike at the financial and economic systems that are directly or indirectly at the heart of the inequality that Black Americans experience: (1) Do nothing; (2) Read more; (3) Adjust income tax withholding; (4) Withhold property taxes; (5) Save more and spend less; (6) Attend more HBCUs and less PWCUs; (7) Discontinue voluntary military service; (8) Produce more physicists and fewer fullbacks; (9) Discontinue supporting professional athletes who do not give back to Black American areas of influence; (10) Eliminate or reorient media consumption; (11) Initiate a Black political party; and (12) Discontinue or reduce support for religious establishments that do not seek to improve conditions in our areas of influence.

If you would take a moment to think about it, then you would find that our notable talking heads and scholars are busy jaw-jacking about the conditions that actually exist: Why we are experiencing adverse conditions; and how we can protest peacefully to create change. Few are pointing to real and workable strategies that can change life's landscape for Black Americans. Is it not about time that we confront situations with realistic, vigorous, and action strategies that can have a real impact on outcomes? Yes! Buckle up for the ride that will take you down avenues of change. However, after you have finished reading this book, your work is not done. It remains up to you to follow through and implement these strategies in your life, and to convince others to do the same.

Strategy 1: Do nothing

In a strategic game there is always a choice to do nothing; i.e., retain the status quo position. Here, "do nothing" means something altogether different—it literally means "do nothing." It is the ultimate rejection of the strategic game itself; that is, do not participate in the game. Black Americans have been engaged in a strategic game in America historically where we have adopted strategies to motivate the larger nation to grant the smaller nation certain concessions. First, eliminating chattel slavery; and second, eliminating "Jim Crow" segregation in favor of civil rights and integration. However, in each case, we were very much willing participants in the game and acceptors of the concessions that were given. Unfortunately, the larger nation always finds a way to permit the concessions, but continue to ensure that, as a whole, the smaller nation is retained as an unequal part of the larger nation. To add insult to injury, the larger nation, because it has the upper hand, is able to parlay the concessions into a stimulus for economic growth for which it is the beneficiary.[4] If Black Americans want to break this cycle of pain and suffering, protests, then concessions, and if we want to stop benefitting the larger nation at our own expense, then one strategy to adopt is to discontinue participating in the game itself. A priori, this

---

[4] As old and new examples of how White America turned concessions to their economic advantage consider the following: (1) A decision to desegregate schools through busing produced very favorable economic outcomes for the companies that manufactured school buses and the related tires that were required for the task, and for the mainly White construction companies that built new schools so that Black and White children could attend school together; and (2) a requirement that police now wear body cameras is creating considerable wealth for the companies that produce these cameras and the related systems. There are many more such examples.

may appear as an impossible strategic action to effect. Is it? What would it mean for the smaller and larger nations?

While a "do nothing" strategic option may appear difficult to effect, it is not impossible. For example, the top 60 percent of Black American households have a median income that is nearly on par with the median White American household income. This 60 percent of Black Americans is not very much dissatisfied with economic outcomes—possibly with the exception of the wealth gap. However, this 60 percent may be convinced that, with income equality, it is just a matter of time before they will be able (in future generations) to achieve wealth equality. Consequently, it may be a difficult proposition to convince these Black Americans that it is in their best interest to reject the game in lieu of a non-guaranteed payoff. What is the payoff?

We have advocated for nation formation—a state that would allow us to control and rule ourselves, to own our land, to educate ourselves, to operate our own government, and to manage our own economy. Do we not deserve to have a nation of our own? Are we less than a nation? Given that the larger nation has refused to welcome all of us with open arms—eliminating racial discrimination and providing real access to economic opportunities—should we not opt for a home of our own that we can transform into a place of peace and prosperity?

Let us assume that the 60 percent satisfaction hurdle is overcome, then what? For certain, the 40 percent, who have been locked out of the mainstream and are in poverty, would opt for nation formation. If near 100 percent cooperation could be achieved in executing the "do nothing" strategy, then there are still questions about the import of such a strategy. How would it work? Would it work?

Given our historical roles in the nation, we find that we occupy important positions in almost all government and commercial operations in the country. A mass sit down strike would place many operations in jeopardy. Depending on the amount of notification given, it might be very difficult for the larger nation to adjust to our absence. This difficulty in adjusting—at least on a short-term basis—may be just the factor that forces the larger nation to listen to our concerns. Logically, the larger nation will want us to continue the cycle of protests and then concessions that can be turned to its advantage, but we should reject such offers and advance our demand for nation-building land and resources.

The first question that is likely to surface in connection with this strategic action is, how will we eat? The answer is that the larger nation is programmed to feed us. It would be a moral disgrace to allow us to starve. Remember that America has an international image that it wishes to maintain. That image would be tarnished forever if the larger nation allowed Black Americans to starve to death or to die without needed medicines. We have legitimate demands that warrant consideration. Therefore, it is reasonable to expect that not many of us would starve under this strategic action.

Of course, Black Americans need to think seriously about operationalizing such a "do nothing" strategy. We would need to determine the timing and the duration. We would want to coordinate this action with other Black people of the world who might have similar grievances to vet against America. In this way, the strategic action could be optimized to strike with maximum effect.

During the "do nothing" strategic action, our objectives should be to "shelter in place" and to seclude ourselves in our areas of influence in order to have little contact with those in the larger nation. We would have to negotiate for food and other amenities, but that action, in and of itself, would symbolize how locked out we have been from commercial and productive processes in America. The extent to which we do not even own grocery stores in or near our areas of influence, the fact that we have little-to-no control of water, power, and sanitation systems that service our areas of influence is a testament to the fact that we remain 21st century slaves in America—with little power or control of the most fundamental aspects of our lives.

Our goals should be to execute this strategy in such a way that the world comprehends our condition and our position in America. Our strategy, not our hope, is that we can leverage this outcome to our own advantage in the form of demanding and receiving land with which to form our own nation so that we can be a people that produces for itself and takes care of itself.

This is a very simple strategy with many complex undertones. However, if Black Americans want to use potentially our final opportunity to get something for self, then we would be well advised to consider this strategy, plan it effectively, and execute it with complete support from every Black man, woman, and child.

Strategy 2: Read more!

If you can read, you can teach yourself to do almost any and everything: From making a cake, to building a house, to building a bomb, and beyond. What does reading more have to do with *21st Century Protests*? A great deal! First, to become an expert at the protests that are suggested herein, you will have to read some of the references that are cited in this volume. Read more. Second, and more generally, if we are to be successful in executing these protest strategies and achieving our ultimate goals, then we must all have an intensified thirst for reading and gaining knowledge. We must want to know more so that we make fewer mistakes in executing our strategies and plans.

There is no need to belabor the point. To become a better athlete, you practice more. To become better entertained, you listen or watch more. To become more knowledgeable, you must read more. Economist say, with a few reservations, more is better. We say, more knowledge is better. To obtain more knowledge, learn to read more!

If Black Americans decide that it is in our best interest to form our own nation and to operate it effectively, then we must learn to produce the goods and services that we need for ourselves. Some of these goods and services we do not now play a role in producing today. In order to learn how to produce these goods and services, we must learn more. Read more to learn more!

Make no mistake: we should not be miseducated—i.e., "educated fools." Rather let us combine obtaining new knowledge by reading with an appropriate amount of contemplation (thinking) so that we are practical, logical, and realistic in our overstanding of the world, what we want from it, and how to obtain it.

Strategy 3: Adjust income tax withholding

The entire argument in this *21ˢᵗ Century Protests Handbook* is to place economic, in this case, financial pressure on the opposition—the US Government. This can be achieved by at least two methods: (1) Withholding financial support, which precipitates the need for the government to borrow more; or (2) cause government to expend more, which, relative to available resources, may also cause government to expand borrowing operations.

Because the US Congress has the "power of the purse," Black Americans have limited control in initiating the second method. In fact, given attitudes about immigration and immigrants, which many argue carries over to the Black population, Congress is very reticent these days to authorize spending that is related to improving Black American well-being. As for the first method, however, Black Americans have the authority to withhold certain financial support from the government under a legitimate tax paying process, but we usually fail to exercise this authority.

On the contrary, due to psychological dependency on the government to help us save for discretionary spending purposes, we usually grant the government access to our hard-earned money free of charge throughout the tax year, with the prospect of receiving a "tax refund," which we then spend lavishly on goods and services that may or may not be in our best interest.

Make no mistake about it, our decision to organize our income tax withholding status by claiming fewer dependents than we are entitled to claim serves as a *defacto* loan to the government, which reduces its need to borrow over the course of the year. In essence, instead of increasing financial pressure on our opponent, we reduce that pressure by adopting this practice.

The discussion thus far builds the case for our third 21st century protest method. Namely, we propose that Black Americans take the time to consider the number of dependents that they are required to claim on their income tax withholding form (W-4). Generally speaking, the Internal Revenue Service (IRS) Code permits a taxpayer to claim a dependent for each person in the household. In addition, depending on household type, taxpayers are allowed to claim an additional dependent if the household is single-headed. As you know, the amount of taxes withheld from income is reduced the greater the number of dependents claimed.

However, many Black American taxpayers intentionally fail to claim the number of dependents allowed on their W-4 Form. Instead, they enter a smaller number of dependents than permitted so that the government withholds more taxes from income. When income tax filing season arrives, Black Americans think that they benefit from this arrangement because they receive a larger "refund" than they would if they had claimed the allowed number of dependents. As already indicated, this is not a "refund" in the strictest sense, but the return of funds that have been loaned to the government on an interest-free basis.

How would the protest work? Under this third *21st Century Protest* method, Black Americans would always claim the maximum number of dependents allowed (being cognizant of the IRS rules). This would reduce the amount of taxes withheld from Black Americans' income during the year and, obviously, refunds would be reduced during tax filing seasons. Therefore, if Black Americans would like to go on a shopping spree (which we advise against) during tax filing season, then we should establish our own saving program—setting aside the funds (preferably in a Black-owned or controlled financial institution) that would have been withheld by the government when fewer dependents were claimed.

How much of an impact would executing this protest have on the pocket books of Black Americans during the course of the year and, consequently, on the government. The answer depends on the extent to which Black Americans have been practicing claiming reduced dependents in the past, and on the extent to which they extend the number of dependents claimed as part of the protest. As an example of the impact, we consider three scenarios in Table 1 (see page 14).

Beginning with the Base Case scenario, we see that the average (mean) household has $51,621 in income (row 1), claims 2 dependents (row 4), and has $4,930 withheld in taxes during a year (row 12). Note that the household may be eligible to claim many more dependents, but refuses to claim the allowed number of dependents in order to amass discretionary savings. In Case 1, the number of dependents is increased to 3, and the amount of taxes withheld during the year is reduced to $4,280—a $650 difference from the Base Case (DIF1 column, row 12). Notice that, if all Black American households fit this scenario, then there would be about a $11.2 billion dollar reduction in the amount of taxes withheld by the national government when the number of dependents is increased to 3 from 2 (DIF1 column, row 11). Finally, in Case 2, the number of dependents is increased to 4, and the amount of annual taxes withheld per household is reduced to $3,629 (row 12). This represents a reduction of $1,300 in annual taxes withheld compared with the Base Case (DIF2 column, row 12). Again, if all Black Americans households fit this scenario, then there would be about a

12

$22.4 billion reduction in the amount of taxes withheld by the national government when the number of dependents is increased to 4 from 2 (DIF 2 column, row 11). Keep in mind that these are prototypical scenarios. Actual scenarios may differ, which could create smaller or larger impacts on the reduction in withheld taxes collected as households increase their dependents to the maximum allowed.

For a Federal Government that borrows literally hundreds of billions of dollars annually, $22 billion does not sound like much. However, $22 billion is significant, and may have other adverse impacts on the national economy. Moreover, state and local income taxes withheld generally follow Federal Government income tax withholding, which means that all levels of government would collect less withholding taxes and would be forced to borrow more. Therefore, the overall impact could be sizeable.

Consequently, we urge those who are organizing protests at the national level to consider motivating Black American households to adopt adjusting their dependents for income tax withholding purposes as just one method for sending a signal to the national, state, and local governments to listen more attentively to our requests for change.

Of course this protest strategy comes with the urging that Black American taxpayers ensure that their tax withholding decisions remain within the letter of the US Tax Code.

Table 1.—Impact of Increased Dependent Claims on Income Taxes Withheld (in US Dollars)

		Base Case (A)	Case 1 (B)	DIF 1 (A-B)	Case 2 (C)	DIF 2 (A-C)
1	Mean Black American annual household income	51,621	51,621		51,621	
2	Biweekly Black American household income	1,985	1,985		1,985	
3	Biweekly health insurance premium	164	164		164	
4	Number of dependents claimed	2	3		4	
5	Amount of income excluded per dependent	167	167		167	
6	Total exclusions based on number of dependents	333	500		667	
7	Taxable income per biweekly pay period	1,488	1,321		1,155	
8	Tax according to 2014 tax table	190	165		140	
9	Total number of Black American households in 2014	17,198,000	17,198,000		17,198,000	
10	Total taxes collected biweekly	3,260,800,332	2,830,764,342	430,035,990	2,400,728,352	860,071,980
11	Total taxes collected annually	84,780,808,620	73,599,872,880	11,180,935,740	62,418,937,140	22,361,871,480
12	Total annual taxes collected per household	4,930	4,280	650	3,629	1,300

Sources: Data on Black household income and the number of Black households are from the US Census Bureau (www.census.gov); data on the health insurance premium are from NBC Television's Washington, DC affiliate (Channel 4) (http://www.nbcwashington.com/news/health/NATL-ACA-328-Average-Monthly-Health-Insurance-Cost-Under-the-Affordable-Care-Act--225324422.html); and information on calculating Federal withholding tax and the related taxable amounts are from Washington State University (http://payroll.wsu.edu/taxes/howto.htm). This information was accessed on the Internet during September of 2015.

14

Strategy 4: Withhold property taxes

This fourth economic protest strategy is based on the fundamental American principle of "no taxation without representation." In this case, we tweak that principle to make it, "no taxation without an appropriate type and level of goods and/or services." In other words, when Black Americans find that they are not receiving goods and services from local governments that are commensurate with the level of taxes being paid, then we should challenge the condition by conducting an economic protest—withholding tax dollars. Understandably, taxes, by definition, are unrequited payments that taxpayers ostensibly agree to make when they are part of the polity. However, the Boston Tea Party makes clear that, in America, it is accepted that an appropriate level of "representation" should be granted, and/or an acceptable level of goods and services should be rendered, by the government that is assessing and collecting taxes. While demonstrations or protests in the form of marches apply certain pressures for change by local authorities, the strategy that we propose should certainly get local officials' attention and should motivate them to act quickly to adopt changes that will result in better delivery of the required goods and services.

Certain important requirements accompany this type of economic protest. First, it must be possible to identify in related state statutes a provision for denial of tax payment in the event of failure to provide appropriate type or level of goods and/or services. Second, the courts must be willing to entertain a case of egregious failure to provide goods/services by government and action by citizen/taxpayers to withhold related taxes.

As a perfect example, we proposed this strategy for Black American taxpayer/citizens in Baltimore, Maryland following riots that ensued after the death of Freddie Gray in 2015.[5] Here is what we proposed.

Although there appeared to be no explicit State of Maryland law concerning denying taxes to a municipality for failure to provide an appropriate type and level of police services, the following sections of the Local Government Articles of the Maryland Annotated Code could have been used to build a case: Section 4-103 (municipalities can be sued); Section 4-311 (funds can be withheld for a cause); Sections 5-302 and 5-303 (a municipality can be liable for certain tortious acts); and Section 21-626 (taxes should not be collected if certain services are not provided).

The strategy that we proposed had three components. First, Black Americans in Baltimore should have sought the aid of the National Associated for the Advancement of Colored People (NAACP, headquartered in Baltimore) legal defense team and/or local lawyers who were willing to petition Baltimore courts for an injunction against the city. The injunction would prevent the City of Baltimore from taking action against Black American citizens who withheld property taxes until issues related to the police department's detrimental and inhuman services were resolved. It seemed reasonable that the court would rule favorably on this issue due to the egregious failures in service delivery by Baltimore's Police Department to areas occupied mainly by Black Americans. The injunction would prevent the city from placing liens or assessing fines, fees, interest, and

---

[5] Freddie Gray was arrested on April 12, 2015 in Baltimore, Maryland for allegedly possessing an illegal switchblade knife. While being transported in the custody of police, he fell into a coma and later died on April 19, 2015. His questionable arrest and treatment while in custody raised and uproar in Baltimore, including riots.

penalties on Black American-owned property when taxes are paid after due dates in connection with this effort.

To be shielded by this injunction, Black Americans would have had to maintain property tax payments in appropriate escrow accounts. This should not have been a problem because most property that is covered by mortgages include escrow accounts that accumulate property tax payments.

Second, after the injunction was in place, Black American property owners would have had to act to withhold property tax payments from the City of Baltimore until issues surrounding detrimental police services were resolved. This would entail writing a letter to a property owner's mortgage company that cites the aforementioned court injunction, and requesting that property taxes not be released to the city until further notice is given.

Third, Black Americans would have had to actively engage the City of Baltimore in sorting out the types of revisions to police services that were required, a process for evaluating the performance of effective services, and a timetable for meeting all requirements. The court should be a part of this process so that it could determine when the city had met its side of the bargain, which would, in turn, motivate a resumption of property tax payments by Black Americans. When the city had fulfilled requirements, then Black Americans could make all tax payments that were due— citing related escrow accounts and, thereby, avoiding repercussions from the city for late payments.

What we know is that money and budgets are critical to policy- and decision-makers at all levels of government. In this particular case, Black Americans comprised over 60% of Baltimore's population. Also consider that Baltimore's 2015 budget was about $3.3 billion; about $0.8 billion of which was associated with property taxes. If Black Americans were responsible for at least one-third of those property tax payments, and if just 25% of Black Americans had participated in the above described strategy, then Black Americans could have withheld over $65 million from Baltimore City coffers over the course of a year. We conclude that this amount would have been sufficient to motivate the city to act quickly to resolve issues related to the provision of police services to Black Americans in the City of Baltimore.

Of course, Freddie Gray's death and the crisis in Baltimore had its own unique details. However, we suggest that there are likely to be many cases today and in the future that could warrant similar action by Black Americans. For example, if local public school officials are not allocating sufficient funds to provide quality education to Black American students, then why should not Black Americans consider withholding taxes that provide the revenue to support public schools? And there are likely to be many more cases where a strategy of withholding property tax dollars could serve as a ready economic protest answer to a problem facing Black Americans all across the nation.

As always, before undertaking this economic protest strategy, due consideration should be given to the unique circumstances involved, to the short- and long-term implications of operationalizing the action, and to how such action is integrated into the overall objectives and goals of Black Americans at the local and national levels.

Strategy 5: Save more and spend less

Surprisingly, academicians reflect controversy over Black Americans' saving behavior. Some argue that, all else being equal, Blacks save more than whites; others argue the reverse—Whites save more than Blacks.[6] This controversy leads us to believe that there is likely some truth to both arguments, and that Blacks and Whites save similar amounts, all else being equal, under particular circumstances. What we know is that past higher incomes and saving behavior have enabled Whites to amass considerably more wealth than Blacks.[7] Therefore, Blacks are hard-pressed to engage in behavior that requires significant financial capital, such as make sizeable investments to initiate businesses or to acquire other financial and/or nonfinancial assets. Thus, our ability to generate new wealth is limited. An inability to generate large volumes of new wealth means that average (mean or median) wealth among the growing Black population will not increase, and that the White-Black wealth gap will persist and is likely to expand.

An expansion of the Black-White wealth gap portends further superimposition of White might over Blacks. In other words, our position as 21st century slaves is not likely to change under status quo conditions. This is untenable and we should do all within our power to ensure that we halt and

---

[6] For example, in the Whites save more corner, we have Marjorie Galenson, (1972), "Do Black Save More?" *The American Economic Review*, Vol. 62, No. 1/2, pp. 211-16. In the Blacks save more corner, we have N.S. Chiteji and Darrick Hamilton, (2002), "Black-White Wealth Gap among Middle-Class Families," *The Review of Black Political Economy*, Vol. 30, No. 1, pp. 9-28.

[7] The US Federal Reserve Board's *Survey of Consumer Finances* reports regularly on the level of wealth possessed by Black versus White households; http://www.federalreserve.gov/econresdata/scf/scfindex.htm.

then reverse the expansion of the Black-White wealth gap. If we do not, we guarantee that future Black generations will be in worse economic condition in America than even we ourselves.

The starting point for changing this potential scenario is to begin to save more. Irrespective of the controversy over Black-White saving behavior, if we are to make progress in growing new Black wealth, we should start with financial assets that we accrue—above and beyond the financial assets that we consume—i.e., we should begin to save more.

This is not to say that Black Americans should become miserly. There is something to be said for acquiring high-quality goods and services when one makes a purchase. There is something to the adage, "It takes money to make money and to save money." That is, an investment in a quality good often means that you save in the long run—as opposed to achieving initial short-term savings by purchasing a cheap product, only to have to dole out more cash when the cheap product fails early. Nevertheless, we should become more circumspect and thoughtful in the purchases that we make. Specifically, we should learn to avoid conspicuous consumption and learn to delay gratification. When you have eaten a meal just an hour or two ago, but you pass a Coca-Cola sign, you should not be motivated to buy and consume a Coca-Cola and chips. If you allow that thought to pass, you may realize, logically, that you really are not hungry after all, and that it was that advertisement that motivated the thought process to buy.

It may sound simplistic, but just changing one's behavior about purchasing sugary soft drinks can save you tens of dollars, if not over a hundred dollars, during the course of a year. Importantly, by discontinuing these purchases, you may improve your health outcomes—which can contribute to saving. Most importantly, you can use the saved resources to invest in an interest drawing bank account, in a small financial security, or in a piece of equipment that will enable you to produce a good for sale.

Multiplying the effects of such changes in behavior can produce marvelous improvements in our saving and, ultimately, in Black Americans' wealth accumulation. Consider that in our young years we discontinued smoking and used the proceeds to purchase our new family's first color television. If, instead of purchasing a television we had used the capital to invest in a financial security, that decision would have resulted by now in, potentially, thousands of dollars of cash. The color television has long failed to work, and we only used it to waste time watching mainly useless programs and sports. The cash would be with us today in order to invest in achieving something more meaningful.

As a nation, we should decide that saving is important. Let us learn to squeeze our pennies a little more tightly so that those pennies turn into dollars, those dollars into tens, hundreds, thousands, millions, and, ultimately, billions of dollars.

If you are behind, and those with whom you are behind are continuing to move forward, then you cannot continue to take the same action and expect to catch up. Rather, you must do something extraordinary to catch up. We know that the gap cannot be overcome in one fell swoop. However, we know that, given the correct motivation and action, we can overcome the Black-White wealth gap. In fact, in 2014, we prepared a brief essay that presents a scenario in which Blacks can surmount the Black-White wealth gap.[8] It is a

---

[8] Brooks B. Robinson, (2014), "From Inequality to Equality: Hypothesizing about the Possibilities," BlackEconomics.org. Accessed on June 24, 2016; http://www.blackeconomics.org/BEFuture/FIE.pdf.

hypothetical scenario; however, the scenario alone is indicative of what can be achieved with appropriate and persistent action.

An important formula to success is realization, motivation, planning, and persistent action. We should realize that there is a problem with negative implications and set a goal for overcoming the problem. We should be motivated to solve the problem by reaching our goal. We should plan precisely and effectively how we intend to reach our goal. And we should engage in persistent action to achieve the goal—despite the odds of success. When we operationalize this success formula, then we can become successful.

What does saving have to do with Black American 21st century protests? Everything. An intent to eliminate the Black-White wealth gap is, in and of itself, a protest statement. The gap should not exist, and we should do all that is within our power to eliminate it. In addition, we may be called upon to use our own resources to fulfill other protest strategies that are highlighted in this book—resources amassed through greater saving. Therefore, a fundamental starting point for 21st century protests is to save and accumulate more wealth so that we can act independently in our own best interest. "Beggars can't be choosers." Beggars can't protest. It takes one with resources to stake out a claim and to fight to attain and maintain that claim. Therefore, if we decide to engage in 21st century protests, then we should, at the same time, decide to save more and build wealth that can be used to operationalize our protest strategies.

Strategy 6: Attend more HBCUs and less PWCUs

We have been crystal clear concerning our perspective on Black Americans' acquiescence to desegregation (integration) as a path for ensuring a reduction in racial discrimination and, ultimately, economic equality in America.[9] In our view, the only reality ensured by desegregation/integration was the superimposition of White (political, educational, and economic) superiority over Blacks. Yes, there has been some upward economic filtering of Blacks at the margin over the last 50 years. However, over 25% of Black Americans remain at the periphery with no hope of upward mobility. A more favorable strategy during the Civil Right Era would have been to opt for resources to use in separate development until Black and White societies were more or less equal, then integration. This principle applies not only to elementary and secondary educational systems, but to tertiary education as well.

Historically Black Colleges and Universities (HBCUs) have suffered greatly due to desegregation/integration. Nevertheless, as we argue in *Understanding Minority-Serving Institutions* in 2008, HBCUs may account for a very small percentage (about 3%) of post-secondary institutions' enrollment, but they account for over 25% of Black students who obtain undergraduate degrees.[10] In addition, HBCU graduates account for 10% of those Black Americans who receive masters, professional, and doctoral degrees. It is no wonder that, for example, Xavier University with a

---

[9] Brooks B. Robinson, (2015), *A Third Freedom*, Black Economics.org, Honolulu, pp. 18-20.
[10] Brooks B. Robinson and Angela R. Albert, Chapter 13, "HBCU's Institutional Advantage: Returns to Teacher Education," in Gasman, Baez, and Turner, Editors, (2008), *Understanding Minority-Serving Institutions*, SUNY Press, New York.

population of about 3,000 students leads the nation in Black graduates who complete medical school.

It is common knowledge that HBCUs offer a much friendlier and unintimidating learning environment than Predominantly White Colleges and Universities (PWCUs). At the same time, it is also clear that PWCUs generally have better facilities and more renowned faculty than HBCUs. Consequently, we must ask the counterfactual, "What would HBCUs look like today if Black Americans had not opted for desegregation, and if appropriate resources had been poured into HBCUs. We all are aware of the rich tradition of Tuskegee University, and how Booker T. Washington and George Washington Carver labored to create a very formidable and productive learning environment using meager resources. Imagine what we would have today if Washington and Carver-type personalities had been at work over the past 60 years pushing HBCUs forward with sufficient financial resources.

There is no doubt that, given sufficient resources and the proper environment, we can be a very creative and productive people. Knowingly, and sometimes unknowingly, we contribute in significant ways to PWCUs; advancing them further, while HBCUs fall further behind. Do not we want something for self—something that we can claim for ourselves and call our own? Would we not do better to place our considerable skills and abilities at the disposal of HBCUs as opposed to giving them so freely to PWCUs, which only treat us badly, use us up, and then replace us with the next flavor of the day?

This is not to say that we should all run away from PWCUs to HBCUs in their current form. HBCUs need to be reorganized and improved in specific ways so that Black intellectual talent can be used most effectively to advance our educational, political, social, and economic causes in America.

What we should realize is that by attending and being employed by PWCUs, we provide them with the economic and intellectual resources that are used to help keep Black America enslaved. The tuition, room, board, and books for which we pay help augment the plant, equipment, and faculty of these institutions. That same plant, equipment, and faculty are used to research and strategize concerning how to maintain the American status quo—which means Black Americans at the bottom of the social hierarchy and every other group above.

Therefore, a critical and impactful Black American protest strategy for the 21st century is to devote as much of our financial and human resources as possible to HBCUs. By so doing, we accelerate the day when HBCUs can produce and provide the type of scientific, political, educational, social, and economic leadership that will ensure our rise in America.

Strategy 7: Discontinue voluntary military service

Historically, Black Americans' participation in the US military reflects strategic thinking. Halting our backwards glance at the Civil War, Black slaves who joined the Union Army were fighting for their own freedom. Black participation in World Wars I and II was aimed at showing White Americans that we could be good citizens—placing our lives on the line—and deserved better treatment at home as a result of facing the risks. Given the marginal improvements in benefits to Blacks and race conditions following World War II, it was reasonable for Blacks to go to the Korean peninsula and take up the fight there. However, by the time we get to Vietnam, it is clear that White America had no intentions of imposing racial equality at home, and the cry came to stay away from Nam.

Since the Vietnam War, Black participation in the US military defies most forms of reasoning. It is true that, since the turn of the millennium, the US military has adopted equipment and procedures that reduce the threat of death in action substantially. However, although the opposition may not be able to kill US troops at will, it has found ways to maim troops horribly. Consequently, you may not die as a US troop abroad, but there is a statistically significant possibility that you may suffer in a variety of ways.

It is also true that, from an economic perspective, there are significant advantages to joining the US military. Because one must possess certain qualifications to join the current US military force, it is probably not accurate to say that military service represents the one chance at a job for many Black soldiers. Nevertheless, it is safe to say that, for those that join the military, it represents an opportunity to generate income, engage in matched saving for education during and after service, and receive considerable housing and health social benefits. In fact, we have concluded from research for a 2012 essay that Blacks who join the military have considerably higher wealth levels than Blacks who have no military service to their credit.[11]

According to the US Department of Defense, there were 227,624 Black Americans serving in the US Armed Forces and Coast Guard at the end of September of 2015—about 17% of the total military Force, but only about 1.2% of the Black labor force. Black participation in the US military has reflected a small, but steady, decline since 2011. What Black Americans should realize is that US military might is what makes America powerful in the world. Consequently, if we want to protest against that power in response to unfavorable treatment at home, we should withhold our service—despite the "benefits" that accrue from service.

A 17% contribution to the US military force is sizable. A loss of this contribution would have a significant impact on the nation's ability to police the world and flash American power at will. It is a contribution that cannot be easily replaced. It seems reasonable that a threat to withhold our participation in the military, in whole or in part, would motivate certain favorable action on the nation's part to convince Black Americans that action can be taken to improve racial conditions in the country. It is worth saying that a call for a boycott of US military service is a risky

---

[11] In an unpublished essay for BlackEconomics.org entitled, "Every Time You Break a Seal," we concluded that "Black respondents with military experience have a $136.9 thousand mean and a $94.2 thousand median wealth advantage over their counterparts who had no military service." These results were derived from our analysis of 2007 Survey of Consumer Finance data that were produced by the US Federal Reserve Board. See Bucks, Kennickell, Mach, and Moore, 2009, *Changes in US Family Finances from 2004 to 2007: Evidence from the Survey of Consumer Finances*, US Federal Reserve Board, Washington, DC.

venture. However, it is one of the most straightforward protests that we could lodge that would likely produce very favorable results for Black Americans.

Strategy 8: Produce more physicists and fewer fullbacks

21st Century Protests emphasizes the importance of breaking historical cycles and shattering stereotypes as a form of protest. There is no better way to do this than to defy a key stereotype that has plagued Black Americans since the beginning of our sojourn in America: We must continue to prove to the world that we have as much or more brain than brawn. We excel at most physical sports that the European has schemed up to occupy the minds of the world, while he walks away with the real prize—control of world's commerce, information, and communications operations. If you control what the world knows, how it communicates, and how it functions, then you have locked up the world and can twist and turn it in any direction that you choose. Unfortunately, we have aided the European in his scheme to control the masses who have been convinced, in many cases, that the most important experience to have is to enjoy sporting events: Football (American and European), basketball, tennis, boxing, baseball, etc. We have helped because we are the most outstanding performers in these sports at all levels. The task that is set before us now is to ween ourselves off of these "pass times," and to re-channel our energies and talent into science, technology, engineering, mathematics, artificial intelligence, robotization (STEMAIR), and other fields that will lead man into the deep future. In a phrase, we need to produce "More Physicists, Fewer Full Backs."[12]

At this time, it is logical for young Black girls and boys in the suburbs and in urban areas to direct their energies into becoming super athletes because they all have a relatively

[12] The author prepared a commentary for TheRoot under this title in 2008. Accessed on June 18, 2016; http://www.theroot.com/articles/culture/2008/09/more_physicists_fewer_fullbacks/.

close associate who has, at a minimum, obtained a full-ride college athletic scholarship. In large urban areas Black youth athletes play with, on a regular basis, colleagues who find their way into the professional ranks at home or overseas. Therefore, it makes sense to develop a mindset that these young Black girls and boys, too, can play college and professional sports. However, as we all know, the odds are very small that they can become superstars and pull down the big multi-million dollar professional contracts that the likes of Lebron James, Stephan Curry, Cam Newton, or Russel Wilson now command.

What these young Black boys and girls should realize first is that they expend a great deal of energy and time in their drive to become great athletes. Second, they should realize that, if they invest the same type of effort in pursuit of becoming proficient at STEMAIR and related fields, then they can expect to achieve greatness in these fields as well. More importantly, they should realize that, at least from a physical point of view, it is much easier to become a physicist as opposed to a fullback. For example, physicists master their craft in the quiet and air-conditioned environs of laboratories and libraries—not out on a 90 degree football field in the dead of summer. In addition, while one can become injured if an experiment goes awry, the odds of this happening are much smaller than incurring a severe leg or head injury on the football field that can scar an athlete for life. Most importantly, yes it is great to hear the crowd roar for a few seconds—maybe even a minute or two—when one scores a touchdown, it is much more gratifying to know that your work as a scientist will live through the ages. For athletes, records are made to be broken, and only the very best athletes are remembered more than a generation. Think about how the world will continue to celebrate for years to come the lives of George Washington Carver, Charles Drew, Granville T. Woods, Vivien Thomas, and Mark Dean—just to name a few. The reality is that the world is already well on the STEMAIR path, and there are new scientific fields on the horizon that will require exploration. We just have to convince our youth that science is the lifeblood of tomorrow's world.

Let's be clear: It is likely that one must be skilled in the sciences in order to conduct protests in the future. For example, it may be necessary to work around common forms of communication in order to reach a protest audience, because common forms of communication may be blocked to prevent such protests. In addition, once Black Americans are able to wrest land from the United States and form our own nation, then it will be critical that we have all of the STEMAIR skills at our disposal so that we can facilitate the smooth physical functioning of that nation. We need the full gamut of STEMAIR scientists if we want to build a nation that meets all of our needs, and can meet the challenges of nation building in the world of tomorrow.

How do we get there from here? By enabling young Black girls and boys to master STEMAIR and related fields. Use the arguments outlined above to convince them that it is in their best interest to become a physicist as opposed to a fullback. If we begin when they are very young, then they will never develop an appetite for sports, but will learn to love science. If we can create a thirst for science knowledge in the hearts and minds of young Black boys and girls, and if we help and support Black youth in acquiring the tools that are required to become masters of the sciences, then we can develop a generation of scientists, who can conquer the world. By so doing, we cannot only actively protest against the old brawn over brain stereotype that has plagued us historically, but we can also move closer to the day when we are truly ready to engage in the ultimate protest against an unfair American system. The ultimate protest action is to depart America and arrive in a land of our own that has all of the implements of life that the modern world can offer, minus the discrimination, hate, and death that has marked our existence in these United States.

Strategy 9: Discontinue supporting professional athletes
who do not give back to Black American areas of influence

Fundamentally, we must ask: "Why are Black Americans so
inclined to support and nurture those who do not have Black
Americans' best interest at heart?" Is this the result of our
slavery experience? It certainly is a slave mentality. Why are
we so unwilling to fight back (protest) when conditions are
rigged in our disfavor and justice is denied? If the rest of the
world is justified in supporting those who support them, and
in fighting for justice when justice is denied, then Black
Americans are justified in committing these same acts. A
perfect circumstance for exhibiting this type of "pro-self"
behavior is with respect to the consumption of sports.

It is one thing to gain physical benefits and pleasure from
participating in sports activities. It is another thing altogether
to devote one's time, energy, effort, and resources to, and
derive pleasure from, observing others participating in
sporting events. Observers have, for some time, pointed their
finger at the Western world and indicted it for using grand
divide-and-conquer schemes to separate indigenous
populations and people of color from untold amounts of their
natural wealth. Have we stopped to consider that each time
we see a sporting event, we are seeing a divide-and-conquer
scheme, in miniature, in action? The sad part about all of this
is that we, Black Americans, are particularly vulnerable to
choosing sides and supporting one team or another when, in
fact, we have no real skin in the game—except for, as we
have said, our time, energy, effort, and resources.

Due to our over emphasis on the physical aspect of life,
which results from long-lasting stereotypes, we enjoy doing
and seeing physical activities more so than mental activities
at this stage. The problem with this picture is that, by and
large, physical activities are less profitable than mental

activities in today's global economy. It is true that there are a few highly selected Black American sports stars who pull down extraordinary sums due to their athletic prowess. The operative term here is "few." But everyone cannot "Be Like Mike."[13] Therefore, it may be logical to pursue sports as a career choice (because everyone knows somebody who has made it to the pros), but it is not rational (because the odds of making it are so small). What is rational is to pursue mental activities (learning, study, research, science, technology, engineering, mathematics, artificial intelligence, and robotization) with a vengeance.

If we discontinue our personal pursuit of sports, then why should we continue to waste time, energy, effort, and resources observing sporting events? If we keep making Lebron James our super hero, when will we reach the point of having other types of super heroes that are relevant for life in the 21st century and beyond?[14] This is particularly poignant for Black super sports heroes who refuse to share and invest their wealth in Black areas of influence that produced them and that support them and their teams.

Observe this reality. Most Black American sports star who pull down significant sums are characterized by the following outcomes: (i) Their caretakers (lawyers, accountants, publicists, etc.) are predominantly White; (ii) they acquire a partner who is White; (iii) they reside in the suburbs; (iv) they invest mainly in White-owned businesses; and (v) they give lip-service to Black areas of influence by providing a few meager grants or scholarships.

---

[13] The reference is to famous National Basketball Association player, Michael Jordan. During 1992, a Gatorade television commercial ran under this "Be Like Mike" theme.
[14] Lebron James is another famous National Basketball Association player, who established himself as an icon during the 21st century.

34

A withdrawal of support from Black super sports stars is not only to punish them and make them accountable to Black areas of influence, but it is also to punish the 21st century slave traders who traffic in human flesh. In our view, there is little difference between the sales receipt that slave masters obtained when they purchased slaves in the *antebellum* period and the contracts that are signed by sports teams with athletes today. Once the ink is dry on contracts, the athletes lose many of their freedoms. If they defy their masters, then they risk ostracization from sports and loss of their livelihood. Consequently, a withdrawal of support from sports is a protest for freedom of all human beings—athletes and non-athletes alike.

However, withdrawal of support for sports is more than a punishment for athletes and their owners and a protest for freedom in general, it is protest for personal freedom. Indeed, once you become addicted to sports, you lose the freedom to pursue an abundance of productive options in life. The time, energy, effort, and resources that are wasted on supporting sports can be directed to innumerable positive endeavors. Too many young men become old men before their very eyes as they keep promising themselves that they will get up and do something, but find themselves locked before the big screen watching Lebron, Steph, Russel, Cam, and Serena.[15]

Even if Black super star athletes identify with, and invest in, Black areas of influence, we should think twice about supporting them. We should seek to supplant the Black "brawn over brain" stereotype with a Black "brain over brawn" mantra that we drive home until we convince

---

[15] The references are to the aforementioned Lebron James; famous National Basketball Association Player Stephen Curry; famous National Football League quarterbacks Russel Wilson and Cam Newton; and world famous tennis player Serena Williams.

ourselves and the world of its truth. We should consider future Black generations and recognize that they will benefit more from mental and intellectual excellence than from athletic excellence.

This new attitude concerning discontinuing support for sports applies to Black entertainers as well. They, too, become slaves to record labels and movie houses when they sign contracts. Let us engage in a 21 century protest and help them obtain their freedom by withdrawing our economic support. Black performers may suffer, but it is better that they suffer in small numbers today than that millions of Blacks suffer in future generations because of the adverse stereotypes that today's Black performers help perpetuate. We address this issue more completely in the next chapter.

Strategy 10: Eliminate or reorient media consumption

Why should Black Americans protest against the media?

Morally, we should protest against the media because it is full of lies and half-truths. Economically, we should protest against the media because its stereotyped presentations of Black Americans costs us billions of dollars each year and causes many of us to have a low self-perception and to think that we are incapable of doing for ourselves.[16]

What we know is that, if they are hungry, people will eat. They will eat garbage if that is all that they are fed. On the other hand, they will eat clean and healthy food, if that is what they are served. In the main, the media feeds the population garbage. However, the power of the media is that it can convince you to eat, even when you are not hungry, and you must eat the garbage that it serves up. Importantly, due to audience segmentation, selected portions of the White population consume a less biased form of media than that consumed by Blacks Americans.

What we also know is that, while the mind is the most powerful instrument in the universe, down here on Earth, minds are controlled by the media. When you have a country with a population of 330 million, which is also the most powerful country in the world (economically and militarily), you cannot afford to leave much to chance. Therefore, you use this powerful tool to control and entrap the minds of that portion of the population that is most susceptible to anger due to the conditions that they face. Consequently, that portion of the population that is absorbed and controlled by

---

[16] Many sources discuss these detrimental characteristics of the media. Consider Brooks B. Robinson, (2009), "Black Unemployment and Infotainment," *Economic Inquiry*, Vol. 47, No. 1, pp. 98-117, and consult the reference section for other relevant sources.

the media is unable to extricate itself from media slavery, think outside of the box (the television), and plan its rise.

When you travel the world, you will see that the American media is ubiquitous. You must think that the adverse stereotypical images of Black Americans that we see in the US are also pervasive around the world. As a result, many people the world over have formed unfavorable opinions of Black Americans. When they meet us in their home countries abroad, and when they come to the US to live, they react to us negatively because of the media images that they have consumed. Thus, the global population is less susceptible to assist us in our rise.

This beast of a machine, the media, is wandering to and fro the earth seeking whom it may devour. Devouring your valuable time that could be spent in productive activity that contributes to your rise; gobbling up your valuable resources as it coerces you to purchase goods and services that you may not be able to afford and that you may not need; and consuming your life with activities that you did not initially intend to perform.

There is just one effective response to being overwhelmed by such a powerful instrument; shut it out of your life. Eliminate, to the extent possible, all (unnecessary) forms of media. And, where you cannot do this, then make every effort to reorient your media consumption behavior by only consuming those forms of media that are unbiased (if you can identify any), and that provide information that enables you to live a more informed life.

Therefore, Black Americans should protest against the media because it is a mechanism that robs us daily of the knowledge, skills, and abilities required to rise from the bottom of American society. If we shut out the media, then media owners may find it worthwhile to transform the images that they project of us. New, fair, and balanced images of Black Americans will enable us to see ourselves and our great capabilities more realistically. The world will come to know who we really are. In combination, these realizations will help enable our rise.

Strategy 11: Initiate a Black political party

For this *21st Century Protests* strategy, we repeat below in its entirety a recently released BlackEconomics.org essay entitled, "Why Not a Black Political Party."[17] It builds arguments for the economic advantages that come with having our own political party, and serves as an automatic form of protest after having labored as political slaves to the Democratic and Republican Parties for over 150 years.

Introduction

This essay is about political parties. We begin with several important questions about political parties, the most important of which may be, "Why is there no Black political party?" Beyond the critical questions, we note two important realities about Black votes. We ask: "Why did earlier efforts to raise a Black political party fail?" In the end, it will take leadership to initiate efforts to organize a Black political party. Therefore, we inquire why notable and relatively wealthy Black Americans have not sought to solidify a legacy for themselves by seeking to raise a Black political party. We end the essay by highlighting what a Black political party may actually be able to accomplish, and we issue a call for this effort to be undertaken in the near term.

From our perspective, the formation of a Black political party is a logical and rational objective that is already in place on a *de facto* basis with little-to-no benefits for the average Black Americans. It seems the right thing to do to formalize a Black political party so that average Black

---

[17] See "Why Not a Black Political Party." Accessed on May 22, 2016; http://www.blackeconomics.org/BEFuture/WNABPP.pdf.

Americans can at least effect positive efforts to gain benefits through a tried and true political process.

Questions that baffle the mind

When a Black American begins to think seriously about political parties in the US, s/he usually gets around to the following two questions:

1. Why aren't there more political parties in the US—a nation that prides itself on democracy, which is supposed to be all about voice?
2. What do political parties do?

The first question is very baffling because so many of the world's democracies operate with few-to-many political parties. The argument has long been that it is easier to get things done with just two parties as opposed to many. The recent history of grid-lock in the American political system calls this argument into question.

As a possible explanation for a two-party system, we surmise that two is a good number for those who want to employ the old tricknology that has worked to bamboozle and hoodwink the world for the last 6,000 years. It is an effective divide-and-conquer scheme. Moreover, when one accounts for the centrist stances that are often adopted in the end by political candidates, essentially, one ends up with a blending of the two political parties; i.e., one basic position on which the polity votes.

The second question is not so baffling, but it appears to be little understood. In the party of the US President and of the two houses of Congress, one has the forces that not only establish the nation's legislative agenda, but often, by default, its economic agenda as well. For Black Americans, who are at the bottom of the nation's economic ladder, it makes sense that we would be very interested in influencing the economic agenda and would, therefore, have a strong interest in influencing political outcomes through the political party process.

But there is a third question, which, given the foregoing, is most baffling:

3. Why isn't there a Black political party?

As already mentioned, it may very well be the goal of the most powerful in the country to restrict political parties to two to give the appearance of choice: A wolf and a fox. In the end, as Malcolm X pointed out, they are both members of the dog family. They have shown historically that they have not had an inherent interest in the best outcomes for Black Americans. Every important legislative economic victory that Black American have won, and there have been only a few, have required considerable sacrifice on our part: Lives lost, physical injury, jail time, protest time, and a scar on our historical psyche. So efforts have always been afoot to thwart attempts to establish or maintain a "third" party— especially a Black political party.

Nevertheless, given a Black population of 40 plus million in 2015, and with over 25 million 18 years or older and eligible to vote, it seems reasonable that we would want to leverage this political power to obtain good for ourselves.[18]   The

---

[18] These statistics were derived from Sandra Colby and Jennifer Ortman, (2015), *Projections of the Size and Composition of the US Population: 2014 to 2060*, Current Populations Report PS25-1143, US Census Bureau. Washington, DC; and from Thom File, (2015), "Who Votes? Congressional Elections and the American Electorate: 1978-2014," *Population Characteristics*, P20-577, US Census Bureau, Washington, DC.

answer to "why there is no Black political party" will come forth as we proceed.

Important and simple realities

The first simple reality comes out of research conducted by Black in 1948.[19] He is credited with having identified the underlying logic of the median vote theorem. It is an important theorem because it characterizes a very favorable outcome for Black Americans. In essence, when all votes are organized along a linear political spectrum, the vote that is at the median (half on one side and half on the other) is the one that carries the day—wins the election. In the US where the Democratic and Republic parties nearly split the total vote (including whites and other ethnic groups—excluding Blacks), the Black vote usually represents the median vote and, therefore, decides most major elections.[20]

Walton makes it abundantly clear that the two major parties and many third parties understood this situation very well.[21] He points out that as early as 1843, the Liberty party appointed Negro delegates to high positions on various committees. The Free Soilers elected Frederick Douglass as Secretary of their 1852 political party convention. The Peoples' or Populists' party and the Progressive party sought actively and vigorously Black membership in the late 19th and early 20th century, respectively. The doctrinal parties (Socialist and Communist) parties found it important to their development to seek to attract Black membership. It goes

---

[19] Duncan Black, (1948), "On the Rationale of Group Decision-making," *Journal of Political Economy*, Vol. 56, No. 1; pp. 23-34.
[20] Of course Hispanics, another important ethnic group in the nation, can argue the same. When the total vote excluding Hispanics is split on a political issue, then Hispanics can claim a median vote position.
[21] Hanes Walton, Jr., (1969), *The Negro in Third Party Politics*, Dorrance & Company, Philadelphia.

without saying that the Republican and Democratic parties have mixed histories concerning their interest in securing Black membership. Nevertheless, when politically expedient, all of these parties resorted to efforts to attract the Black vote. Therefore, Black's theorem was well understood long before he espoused it, and remains so today.

Given our advantageous position in the political strategic game, it makes sense that Black Americans would want to isolate ourselves to maintain our median voter position. One of the best ways to do this is to form our own political party, and to use that political party to leverage that median vote to secure the related benefits that can be secured.

The second simple reality is that Black Americans have essentially acted as our own political party historically. That is, Blacks have been nearly monolithic in our voting—either voting for the Republican Party, when it was the party of Lincoln and later for the Democratic Party, as the party of Roosevelt, Kennedy, Johnson, Carter, Clinton, and Obama. In other words, we vote mainly as a bloc, which is consistent with voting by political parties. For example, in 2012, 76% of Black Americans polled indicated that they were democrats; 5% said they were Republicans; 16% were Independent; and 3% were affiliated with other political parties or did not know their affiliations.[22] When we form our own political party, voting as a bloc is likely to continue. The important change will be that we will have operationalized an organizational structure that can leverage more effectively the power of our voting bloc.

Forming a Black political party and voting as a bloc may seem anomalous in light of the nearly 50-year trend of the

---

[22] Pew Research Center, (2012), *A Closer Look at the Parties in 2012*, Washington, DC. Accessed on August 5, 2016; http://www.people-press.org/2012/08/23/a-closer-look-at-the-parties-in-2012/.

four-way disintegration of Black America.[23] We believe that this trend is by design. However, we can design an effort to reverse the trend. Is it not logical that we look into the future and envision a path that is most favorable for us? Political strength is in numbers. Therefore, we should see the future benefit of leveraging our growing population and median voter status, and make a decision to form a Black political party that can produce the benefits that we desire.

Why earlier efforts to raise a long-standing Black political party failed?

Beginning in earnest in the early 1960s, Black political parties in their two varieties (parallel/satellite and independent parties) sprung up to give voice to Black Americans' fundamental rights and critical needs. Walton does a superb job of chronicling the rise and disappearance of these parties.[24] They focused mainly on local and state politics: e.g., the Mississippi Freedom Democratic Party (MFDP); the Lowndes County Freedom Organization (LCFO, also known as the Black Panther Party); and the National Democratic Party of Alabama (NDPA).[25] Who can forget Fannie Lou Hamer's exploits at the 1964 Democratic National Convention in Atlantic City, New Jersey. However, probably the most instrumental personality in the rise of these political parties was Stokely Carmichael (aka Kwame Ture) who, *inter alia*, coined the phrase "Black Power" as

---

[23] See Eugene Robinson's 2010 analysis of the four primary Black American groups in *Disintegration: The Splintering of Black America*, First Ancho Books, New York.

[24] Hanes Walton, Jr., (1972), *Black Political Parties*," The Free Press, New York.

[25] The Black Panther Party mentioned here is different from the Black Panther Party for Self Defense that was founded in 1966 in Oakland, California by Huey P. Newton.

part of his efforts to build support for Black political parties in Mississippi.

Moving forward to the late 1960s and the early 1970s, Black political parties with strong national interests surfaced. The most notable of these parties were the Peace and Freedom Party and the National Black Political Convention, which led to the formation of the National Black Political Assembly. While the latter was well-organized and attracted significant support (at least initially), only the former actually placed Black candidates on presidential ballots.[26]

Walton reveals that a lack of political maturity on the part of the parties' members prevented each of these Black political parties from achieving significant longevity.[27] In combination, a failure to attract enough Black votes, the absence of sufficient financial support, internal conflicts and defections, and changing times (mainly integration of the American society including political parties) caused Black political parties to dissolve, align with other third parties, or merge with the two major political parties.

It could be argued that the latter reasons is the most important contributor to the demise of Black political parties. It is true that all of these Black political parties had as a *raison d'être* opening doors to Black political participation in the nation. Once the nation began to soften on permitting Black participation in political affairs, the primary reason for the existence of Black political parties faded.

But, as always, things change as time elapses. In this case, Black Americans now have new strategic political,

---

[26]The Peace and Freedom Party placed Eldridge Cleaver and Ronald Daniels on presidential ballots in 1968 and 1992, respectively.
[27] Op. cit., Walton, Jr. (1972).

46

economic, and social interests and, therefore, have new reasons for forming a Black political party. Therefore the operative question is: "How do we raise one?"

Want to leave a legacy?

The difficulties that were experienced historically in raising and sustaining a Black political party should not disparage current-day leadership that is interested in optimizing political outcomes for Black Americans. In fact, it seems reasonable that selected relatively wealthy Black Americans who have dabbled in politics as important promoters of candidates should have a desire to solidify their legacies in this life by collaborating to raise a Black political party today.

Think of Oprah Winfrey, Richard Parsons, Kenneth Chenault, Russell Simmons, Jay-Z, and Beyoncé. Add in a few wealthy athletes such as LeBron James, Michael Jordan, Magic Johnson, and up-and-comers, such as Stephen Curry, Cam Newton and Russell Wilson. Together, they represent a solid base for gathering the finances and the wherewithal to start a process of raising a Black political party. Add in Cathy Hughes, and we organize access to at least a couple of television networks and a radio network to use to publicize the effort. What greater legacy would one want to leave behind, which could (like the current Democratic and Republic Parties) stand for well over 150 years.

It is nearly impossible, today, to evolve the type of legacy that has been left to us by the likes of Paul Cuffee, Gabriel Prosser, Denmark Vesey, David Walker, Nathaniel Turner, Frederick Douglass, Booker T. Washington, W.E.B. DuBois, Marcus Garvey, Elijah Muhammad, Rosa Parks, Malcolm X, or Martin Luther King, Jr. However, by making an effort to raise a Black political party, the aforementioned wealthy Black personalities of today could defy the status quo and strike a blow for securing rights and benefits for Black Americans.

We should not be confused that a Black Political Party can or should emerge in full bloom. We should recall that in 1854, today's Republican Party began with a gathering of a few committed activists in a one-room school house in Ripon, Wisconsin. Consider the party's power today. Similarly, a Black political party can grow, over time, into a powerful instrument, which can wrest from the political process in this country the types of benefits that we so richly deserve.

To achieve such growth, the Black American body *politique* cannot afford to sit and do nothing. If wealthy Black Americans light the political party fire, then every eligible Black American voter should keep the fire burning by being a card-carrying party member, and should reflect political maturity by contributing financially and politically to the party on an ongoing basis.

What can a Black political party do?

In short, the answer to this question is: "The same things that the two major political parties can do, but probably on a smaller scale." After some thought, we arrived at four important objectives that a Black political party might achieve—at a minimum.

1. Create what Black America needs most: Operational jobs as well as jobs in the broader economy. In other words, a Black political party must have operational staff members across the nation. More importantly, assuming that the party is able to operate effectively, it should be able to influence social and economic

policies in order to create continuously a significant supply of new jobs for Black Americans in the broader economy.

2. Linked to the first objective, a Black political party should be able to create leverage for Black Americans and enable us to obtain more of the benefits that we desire from the US political, economic, and social systems. Critical to this objective, a well-organized party should enable us to punish politically those who defect from the political strategy that we establish for ourselves.

3. Linked to the second objective, a Black political party should help us to assemble a structure that can facilitate the formulation and monitoring of a long-term, political, economic, and social strategic plan— something that have been sorely missing from our play in the national strategic game from the outset.

4. As an excellent side-benefit, a Black political party should enable us to extend our knowledge concerning how to operate political systems in the event that we found a nation of our own at some point in the future.

If a Black political party satisfies all or most of these objectives, then it would have been well worth its creation. As already discussed, we have a history of creating political parties, and even managing major political parties in the US. For example, Ron Brown served as Chairman of the Democratic National Committee in the late 1980s and early 1990s and was instrumental in securing the presidency for Bill Clinton. More recently, Michael Steele served as Chairman of the Republican Party during 2009-2011. Consequently, achieving the aforementioned objectives should not be new territory. Rather, the creation and sustainment of a Black political party will mark the first time that we will fulfill these objectives strictly for ourselves as an important and significant player on America's political stage.

In a political world where million-dollar donors and political action committees rule the day, only large actions influence outcomes significantly.[28] A large action that Black Americans can implement to influence outcomes is to organize ourselves as a political party and to throw our political weight around as a sizeable voting bloc. Failure to adopt this approach may effectively limit considerably our voice in American politics despite possessing over 20 million eligible votes and serving as the median voter.

Now is the time

Too often in the market place of ideas concerning Black Americans those participating in the dialogue pose problems without proposing solutions. In this case, the problem is that Black Americans are not benefiting politically as we should because we are not leveraging our median voter status. This essay proposes that we solve this problem, at least in part, by establishing a Black political party. The party would enable us to organize ourselves and establish a formal structure that should permit us to bargain with the powers that be—our votes in exchange for political, economic, and social benefits that we choose.

---

[28] See Nicholas Confessore, Sarah Cohen, and Karen Yourish, (2015), "Small Pool of Rich Donors Dominate Election Giving," *The New York Times*, August 1st, Accessed on August 5, 2015; http://www.nytimes.com/2015/08/02/us/small-pool-of-rich-donors-dominates-election-giving.html?_r=0; and Tim Higgins, (2015), "Million-Dollar Donations Fuel Super-PAC's New Dominance," *Bloomberg*, July 31st, Accessed on August 5, 2015; http://www.bloomberg.com/politics/articles/2015-08-01/million-dollar-donations-fuel-super-pacs-new-dominance.

Of course, obtaining these forecasted results depends, in large measure, on the quality of our leadership. Organizing and sustaining a Black political party is no guarantee that these benefits will accrue. In other words, establishing a Black political party must be part of a broader indicator that we have achieved a certain degree of political maturity—including the ability to hold our leadership accountable.

It is our choice whether we take responsibility for making a Black political party a reality. Casual observation will tell us that other minority groups are leaning in this direction. If we and the broader nation stand by idly, we will find that not only have Hispanics formed their own political party, but that they will have also rewritten completely the political demographic landscape in the form of Latinofornia, New Latinico, Latinizonia, Latinexas, and Latinorida.[29] We are already close to the point where we look up after two generations and find that another immigrant group has entered the US at the bottom of the socio-economic ladder and has found its way completely around us to a superior political, economic, and social position. If we are wise, then we will not allow this to occur, but will form our own political party, and then leverage it to elevate our own position.

Time is moving on. The 2016 election is around the corner. Let us not let it pass without at least a serious discussion about forming a Black political party. Let us establish as a goal that 2020 should not come and go without the

---

[29] It was recently announced in the press that Hispanics now exceed whites in the State of California. See Javier Panzar, (2015), "It's Official. Latinos Now Outnumber Whites in California," *Los Angeles Times*, July 8th. Accessed on July 19, 2015; http://www.latimes.com/local/california/la-me-census-latinos-20150708-story.html.

realization and operationalization of a Black political party. The time for action is now!

Strategy 12: Discontinue or reduce support for religious establishments that do not seek to improve conditions in our areas of influence

In the United States, you can obtain data on almost everything. However, Black American religious organizations are very reticent to provide information concerning the donations that they receive. What we know is that Black American religious organizations are notorious for building new structures that are not very productive. They are used on Sunday mornings and possibly one or two nights per week for religious services; otherwise, they lie idle. Economists would call church structures inefficient capital investment. What we also know is that much of the Black religious leadership does quite well financially—benefitting from tithes and offerings and gifts in the form of homes, cars, and so much more. The question that Back Americans should ask is: What physical benefit is the church providing to you individually and to the broader Black American areas of influence? Do they create good, high-paying jobs? Do they produce anything other than entertainment in the form of religious services?

Some will respond that we are missing the entire point. They will say that church and religion are about guidance concerning living this life so that one can go to heaven, as opposed to hell, in the afterlife. We are not religious scholars; however, we question whether a benevolent God would permit your birth into this world, free will to enjoy the "good things" of life, but then punish you after death because you commit acts, the morality of which are a matter of debate and contention by various religious groups. It appears more logical to us that karmic law would be more readily in play, and that one would receive one's just desserts in this life—according to one's own actions. But we digress.

The point that we are making with this 12th 21st century protest strategy is to suggest that Black Americans discontinue engaging in inefficient and ineffective investment. Yes, contributing to a religious organization is an investment. Based on your money contributions to a religious organization (investment), you may expect to receive the benefit of being given a petty position or title (deacon, mother, choir director, officer of the church, etc.), and the right to have your dead body lie in state after death for a funeral service. Our contention is that there are many more meaningful and productive ways of garnering these benefits without such an enormous investment. You can achieve status or a title as part of a nonpaying or minimal paying club, and your body can lie in state at the mortician establishment as part of the total funeral services package. Therefore, the thousands of dollars in investment that you make at your local religious establishment can be better expended to save for a business that you might wish to embark upon; create a financial investment in a Black-owned institution that provides returns; finance your education or that of your children or grandchildren; acquire physical assets that can be of benefit to you and others; or to be placed in a fund that will be awarded to your heirs after death.

Certain Black American religious organizations, on the other hand, use contributions that they receive to provide educational services and/or scholarships; produce goods and services that are sold to the public and create jobs in the process; create funds that can be the source of loans to membership for a variety of purposes; and distribute goods, services, or scholarships to those who are truly in need. In these cases, it makes sense to support such organizations. Unfortunately, it is rare to find that Black religious organizations are conducting affairs in these ways.

When we find that Black American religious organization are not engaging in productive actions for our areas of influence, then we should withhold our investments in these organizations and redirect them to more productive purposes. Quite often, in the political arena we hear calls for Black Americans to reach a higher level of political maturity by being able to hold our politicians accountable. It seems to us that it is high time for Black Americans to begin to show greater religious maturity which will be evidenced by our ability to hold our Black religious leadership and organizations accountable.

Moreover, we know that the larger society comprehends the importance, in fact the centrality, of Black religious organizations in our areas of influence. The larger, White, society relies often on Black religious organizations as an avenue to reach the Black American populace. By rejecting nonproductive Black religious organizations, we reject the broader society's efforts to keep us in check.

But, as emphasized earlier, we should not simply discard Black religious organizations and expend foolishly our former contributions to them. Rather, we should strategize on how we can leverage the resources that we formerly committed to the Black church to productive and useful purposes.

Although there is no readily available and confirmed estimate of the amount of funds that Black religious organizations receive each year, by deduction, we conclude that the amount is well into the billions of dollars. Now let us realize that redirecting these billions of dollars from virtually nonproductive purposes to more productive purposes would be considered by the larger society to be a strong economic protest strategy—one that could be very harmful to them, but very beneficial for us.[30]

---

[30] Consider that White American construction firms build most of the Black churches that are constructed, and that White American financial institutions benefit greatly from the flow of contributions into church bank accounts. Also, White American firms produce most of the implements of religious worship: From clerical collars, to choir robes, to hymn books, to musical instruments that are used for worship. Probably as important, if not more important, White American retail establishments sell most of the "Sunday go to meeting" clothes and shoes that Black Americans purchase.

Conclusion

The 12 21st century protest strategies discussed herein are broad in nature. They must be altered and tailored to the unique circumstance that motivates each new protest and other economic protest strategies must be devised. However, all of these conditions are central ingredients for fashioning 21st century protests.

Which brings us to the need for another component of 21st century protest strategies. This necessary component arises because Black America has allowed our protests to ebb and flow historically—the result of our failure to be strategic in planning protests. We have not seen, nor motivated, the need for persistence in protests. As part of the proposed new strategies going forward, there should be an attempt to undertake sustained pressure on the system through protests. We should not await a crisis to mount protests in turn. If we do, then there will be long lulls in advancement of our agenda. The opposition knows well how to alter its behavior to reduce its harsh tactics and transform its efforts to stifle our rise. Rather, our actions should be based on long-term and persistent 21st century, economic-based protest strategies that are designed to keep the opposition off balance, losing ground, and acquiescing toward our goals.

The karmic laws of the universe say that we are right in our desire to rise and that we shall win. But we should not stand by idly awaiting karma to materialize. We must be busy implementing the 12 21st century protest strategies that have been highlighted—and others that will, undoubtedly, be devised. If we are intent on being right, if we really want to win, and if we are sincere in implementing 21st century protest strategies effectively, then we will be the beneficiaries of self-fulfilling prophesy. We will be right, we will win, and we will rise!

Epilogue

So our scientists are able to ordain our future goals and objectives, and they are able design a strategic plan that utilizes the 21st century, economic-based protests suggested herein to help us achieve them. Nevertheless, there remains a unique requirement that will determine our success. What is it? A sense of oneness and brotherhood/sisterhood. This may seem particularly difficult to overcome because, as we know, there are now at least four Black Americas. We have permitted ourselves to be divided and conquered many times over. We must decide that our individual and collective futures and the futures of our posterity are more important than the factors that divide us. We need to enter into an "Us and We" paradigm where all that matters is our current and short- and long-term future well-being.

Actually, entering into this paradigm is not as difficult as you might think. We are very cognizant of the differences that separate us. In the past, we may have made special efforts to point out these differences in an effort to magnify them and widen the chasm between us. One or more of us wanted to be "better" than one or more others of us. Now we simply need to reverse that process. Each time that we identify a difference, we must make a concerted effort to reduce and minimize it because we understand that it is a barrier to complete and total success.

We must realize that no one is coming in the clouds to rescue us. We must be invested in the "Us and We" paradigm so that we can focus our energies and efforts to rescue ourselves. It is this new mentality—generated in the ether— that can descend upon us from on high and make us successful in positioning our David-like stature so that we can defeat the Goliath that oppresses us.

The "Us and We" paradigm along with 21st century protests can help us reach our goals and engender for us a place of peace and prosperity into perpetuity.

www.ingramcontent.com/pod-product-compliance
Lightning Source LLC
Chambersburg PA
CBHW071113280526
45787CB00003B/1012

9 781535 161350